Pudge Pig's COUNTING BOOK

By Amye Rosenberg

A GOLDEN BOOK · NEW YORK

Western Publishing Company, Inc., Racine, Wisconsin 53404

This is Uncle Hog's Sweet Shop. One day while he was downstairs unpacking boxes, Little Pudge was left to run the shop all by himself. His first customer was Ruby Rabbit.

"I'll have one raspberry pop, please," she said.

Pudge handed her a big red pop and said,

1

FOR

1

The turtle twins ordered two chocolate tarts.
"We love chocolate tarts," said the turtles.
Pudge smiled and said,

2

FOR

2

Three ducks waddled to the donut jar and quacked,
"Donuts for dessert, please,"
Pudge gave them each a donut and said,

3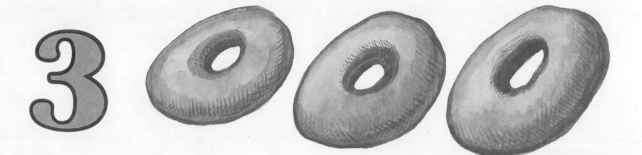

FOR

3

Four giggly gophers wanted gumdrops.
"Yumdrops, gumdrops," they giggled.
Pudge giggled too, and said,

4

FOR

4

Five hedgehogs bounced in.
"We want gingerbread houses!" they shouted.
Pudge opened the cookie case and said,

5

FOR

5

Six merry mouse musicians sang,
"Six cherries in spice for six merry mice."
Pudge liked their song and sang back,

6

FOR

6

Seven big bears wanted barrels of butterscotch.
Pudge lifted the big barrels onto the counter.
It was hard work. He said,

7

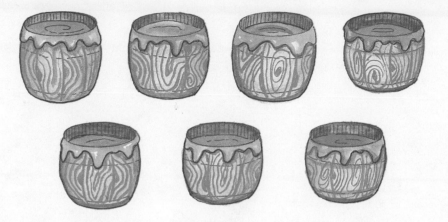

FOR

7

Eight elephants crowded into the tiny shop.
"We want ice cream sundaes," they all said at once.
That was a big job for a little pig, but Pudge
went to work, and cheerfully said,

8

FOR

8

Nine kittens tumbled in and meowed,
"We want candy canes."
  Pudge counted out one for each of them. He said,

9

FOR

9

Uncle Hog came back upstairs. He was very
pleased with the good job Pudge had done.
"You have earned something special," he said to
Pudge. "Take any ten treats you want."
Pudge was so happy, he squealed,